desserts

written by malcolm Long
photography by stillview

KUDOS

Published by Kudos, an imprint of Top That! Publishing plc,
Copyright © 2005 Top That! Publishing plc
Tide Mill Way, Woodbridge, Suffolk, IP12 IAP, UK. www.kudosbooks.com
Kudos is a Trademark of Top That! Publishing plc

contents

introduction

There are those of us who love to cook, and there are those for whom cooking is a chore. However, often even the most reluctant cooks love to produce desserts. There is something a little bit naughty, even decadent about the ingredients used. The blending of butter and cream, eggs and sugar, exotic fruit and spices is all delicious and very fattening – but everyone deserves some self-indulgence.

Desserts can excite the most faded palate, whether it is the richness of a hot sticky toffee pudding on a winter's day, or the lightest chilled lemon soufflé to lift the heaviest meal. Desserts can be warming, satisfying, exotic and exciting but, most of all, fun to make.

Simplicity is the key to nearly all good desserts; simple, good quality ingredients, mixed with care, following the most basic of methods. Simplicity is also the key to this book since it contains recipes which are delicious but easy to make.

Acknowledgments

All food produced by Malcolm Long (Advanced Practitioner) at Colchester Institute, UK, (a government designated centre for vocational excellence). Grateful thanks to the management and staff of the Colchester Institute Centre of Hospitality and Food Studies UK for their help and co-operation in the production of this book, in particular Mr Neil Rippington, Head of Centre and Sarah Scott for her secretarial skills.

basic ingredients

It is always advisable to use the best quality ingredients you can find. Butter, for example, will always taste better than margarine, and flavour is paramount.

Try not to use imported, hot house fruit out of season; not only is it very expensive but it always lacks flavour. Fresh strawberries and raspberries picked locally (or, better still, from your own garden) in the middle of summer taste wonderful and you barely need to touch them to create something really special. In most recipes you can interchange the fruit to suit what is available.

Citrus fruit such as oranges, lemons and limes are often treated with wax to improve the keeping quality. However, this wax is not good to eat, and since much of the fruit flavour is in the skin or zest, this toxic material should always be scrubbed off before use. Citrus fruit will always yield more juice if it is ripe and gentle warming before squeezing will give out yet more.

There are several types of sugar which are used for desserts. Caster sugar is finer than granulated sugar and is used in most cakes, pastries, puddings and biscuits. This sugar is by far the best for normal white meringue and for when you need a sugar which dissolves quickly.

Icing sugar is white sugar ground to a fine powder and is used for icings, cake decorating and for dusting before and after cooking. It is also useful to combine with purées of fruit to sweeten coulis and sauces.

The eggs used in these recipes, unless stated otherwise, are medium and refer to chickens' eggs of approximately 60 grams.

Always test eggs for freshness. A fresh egg placed in cold water will sink to the bottom. If the egg is slightly less fresh it will start to rise towards the surface with the round side uppermost. The higher the egg floats, the older it is, and if the egg floats clear to the surface it is probably bad.

Double cream is the most versatile of all creams; it can be poured, whipped and piped. It is the best cream for cooking but with its minimum butterfat content of 48 per cent, it can be heavy and lack volume unless mixed with single cream before whipping.

Whipping cream has a butterfat content of 35 per cent and is excellent to pipe; it will whip to double its volume so it is quite economical to buy.

Single cream is ideal for pouring. It has a fat content of 18 per cent. However, it will not whip and can split if cooked.

Dry ingredients should always be stored in airtight, clean containers which are labelled and dated, since many ingredients deteriorate with age. Always use up old ingredients first and never add new to old.

Try to buy more dry goods than you intend to use so that you steadily increase the variety of ingredients that you hold. It is always frustrating to find you are unable to make the recipe you choose because you're missing a vital ingredient.

There are times in our busy lives when we have to compromise and, although it would be nice if we always had the time to make everything ourselves, much time can be saved by purchasing ready-made items. Most supermarkets sell ready-made pastry of various types which will speed up preparation times.

Many fruit purées, sauces and coulis are available off the shelf and although it is wonderful to make your own ice creams and sorbets, there are hundreds of excellent varieties available to purchase. There are also many varieties of tinned or frozen fruit available when fresh is unobtainable, and these can be kept in the store cupboard for emergencies.

In terms of equipment, several of these recipes use silicone paper. However, greaseproof paper is a perfectly good alternative. Other things you might need include a piping bag, baking beans (or you can substitute rice or lentils) and a selection of pans, baking dishes and serving plates.

basic conversions

Temperature and weight conversions featured in the following recipes are all approximate. Use the same measurement conversions throughout your recipe to retain the correct ratios.

oven temperatures		
Gas Mark	**Fahrenheit**	**Celcius**
¼	240	115
½	265	130
1	290	145
2	310	155
3	335	170
4	355	180
5	380	195
6	400	205
7	425	220
8	445	230
9	470	245

weights & measurements		
Ounces	**Grams**	**Cups**
1	30	⅛
2	60	¼
3	85	⅓
4	115	½
5	140	⅝
6	170	¾
7	200	⅞
8	225	1
9	250	1⅛
10	285	1¼
11	310	1⅜

banana Lucullus

ingredients

juice and zest of 3 oranges

juice of 2 lemons

30 g (1 oz) flaked almonds

45 g (1½ oz) butter

45 g (1½ oz) demerara sugar

4 bananas

2–3 tbsp orange brandy to taste

2 egg whites

115 g (4 oz) caster sugar

serves 4

1. Remove the zest from the oranges and using a sharp knife, shred very finely into strips. Blanch this in boiling water for approximately 30 seconds and drain.

2. Carefully squeeze the juice from the oranges and add the juice from both lemons. Try to retrieve as much juice as possible from both.

3. Toast the flaked almonds in a dry non-stick frying pan until they start to colour and then tip into a small bowl. Add the butter to the hot pan and, when melted, add the demerara sugar. Gently cook the two together until the sugar melts and begins to caramelise, add the citrus juice and the zest.

4. Cook until the sauce begins to thicken slightly and add the almonds. Turn the heat down low and add the four peeled whole bananas, allow them to poach gently on one side for 3–4 minutes, then gently turn over and repeat the process on the other side.

5. Add the orange brandy to the syrup before removing the bananas. Place each banana in a crescent dish and pour the orange and almond syrup over each.

6. Whisk the egg whites in a clean bowl with a pinch of the caster sugar. When they are stiff, beat in most of the remaining caster sugar until the whites are thick and silky, keep back a little sugar to sprinkle over the top.

7. Using a piping bag and a medium star nozzle tube, pipe the meringue neatly over the bananas and scatter with remaining sugar.

8. Place the bananas in the bottom shelf of a hot grill until they are glazed and golden brown. Serve hot with a ball of vanilla ice cream on each or double cream if preferred.

sticky toffee pudding

ingredients

For the pudding:

90 g (3 oz) dried dates
(stones removed)

100 ml (⅕ pt) boiling water

½ level tsp bicarbonate of soda

45 g (1½ oz) unsalted butter

75 g (2½ oz) caster sugar

1 medium egg

45 g (1½ oz) flour

45 g (1½ oz) self-raising flour

For the toffee sauce:

105 g (3½ oz) demerara sugar

60 g (2 oz) butter

75 ml (2½ fl oz) double cream

vanilla essence

serves 4

To make the pudding:

1. Soak the dates in boiling water, allow to cool.
   Add bicarbonate of soda and mix in a
   food processor.

2. Cream the butter and sugar together and beat in the
   egg. Carefully fold in both flours and mix in the
   cooled date mixture to form a sloppy dough.

3. Pour the mixture into a medium well-buttered
   pudding basin and cover the top with silver foil,
   seal the edges and place in an oven preheated
   to 360°F/185°C/gas mark 4 for approximately
   30–40 mins or until firm to the touch.

To make the toffee sauce:

1. Mix all the ingredients together in a small thick-
   bottomed saucepan and heat until simmering.

2. Cook until toffee-coloured.

To serve:

1. Tip the pudding into a deep-sided, heatproof dish
   and pour over the hot toffee sauce.

2. Place the dish under a hot grill for a few seconds to
   allow the toffee sauce to bubble.

3. Serve with double cream or vanilla ice cream.

baked rice pudding

ingredients

550 ml (1 pt) milk

45 g (1½ oz) pudding rice

30 g (1 oz) butter

60 g (2 oz) sugar

grated nutmeg

vanilla essence

serves 4

1. Boil the milk in a thick-bottomed pan, wash the rice and sprinkle it into the milk.

2. Add half the butter, stir until the milk starts to boil again.

3. Simmer for 3–4 minutes and transfer into a buttered pie dish. Sprinkle with sugar, dot with remaining pieces of the butter and dust with freshly grated nutmeg.

4. Make sure the edges of the dish are clean and transfer into the top of the oven 150°C/300°F/gas mark 2. Cook until a rich brown skin forms on the top and the rice is cooked through (about 1–1½ hrs).

creole rice with glazed apricots

ingredients

900 ml (1½ pt) milk

90 g (3 oz) Carolina or short grain rice

30 g (1 oz) butter

90 g (3 oz) caster sugar

3 eggs

10 slices tinned pineapple

10 tinned apricots

60 g (2 oz) apricot jam

1. Boil the milk in a thick-bottomed pan and sprinkle in the rice. Bring back to the boil and simmer gently.

2. Add the butter and half the sugar. When the rice is nearly cooked, remove from the heat.

3. Whisk the eggs with the remaining sugar. When the rice has cooled slightly, whisk in the beaten eggs.

4. Line the sides of a buttered ovenproof dish with pineapple slices and pour in the rice mixture.

5. Cook in a tray filled with water in a moderate oven 175°C/350°F/gas mark 4 for approximately 30 minutes or until the rice is set.

6. Arrange the apricot halves in the rice and glaze with hot apricot jam boiled with a little apricot juice. Best served warm.

serves 6

bread and butter pudding

ingredients

½ stick of French bread (slightly stale)

60 g (2 oz) butter

45 g (1½ oz) sultanas

30 g (1 oz) caster sugar

fresh nutmeg

30 g (1 oz) apricot jam

For the custard:

135 g (4½ oz) eggs

60 g (2 oz) caster sugar

vanilla essence

550 ml (1 pt) milk

serves 4

To make the custard:

1. Whisk the eggs, sugar and vanilla essence together. Then slowly add the milk, whisking all the time.

To make the pudding:

1. Slice the bread into thin even rounds. Lightly butter each slice and lay in a buttered pie dish in a neat overlapping pattern. Sprinkle with sultanas.

2. Partly cover the bread slices with some of the custard.

3. Leave to stand to allow the custard to soak in, then add the rest of the mixture and dredge with the caster sugar. Grate a little fresh nutmeg over the surface.

4. Wipe the edges of the dish and stand in a pie dish half filled with water. Bake at 175°C/350°F/gas mark 4 for approximately 45 mins–1 hr or until the custard is set and the bread is golden and crusty.

5. When the pudding has cooled slightly, brush with a little apricot jam which has been melted with a little water. Best served warm.

Apricot fritters with hot apricot sauce

ingredients

120 g (4 oz) flour

150 ml (5 fl oz) milk

30 ml (1 fl oz) oil

1 pinch of salt

30 ml (1 fl oz) egg white – from approx. 2 eggs

16 tinned apricot halves in natural juice

60 g (2 oz) icing sugar

small jar of apricot jam

serves 4

1. Sieve the flour, gradually beat in the milk to produce a smooth batter.

2. Stir in the oil and the salt.

3. Cover with clingfilm and allow to rest.

4. Beat the egg white until stiff and gently fold into the batter when required.

To cook:

1. Pre-heat deep fat frier to approximately 180°C/355°F.

2. Dust the apricot halves with a little flour and dip them into the batter.

3. Lift out with a fork and carefully place in the hot fat, fry gently until the batter is golden and crisp. Lift out onto kitchen paper to drain.

4. Dust with icing sugar and serve with hot apricot sauce, made by boiling the apricot jam with a little of the fruit juice and straining into a sauce boat.

cabinet pudding

ingredients

For the custard:

3 medium eggs

45 g (1½ oz) sugar

vanilla essence

400 ml (⅔ pt) milk

For the filling:

30 g (1 oz) glacé cherries

90 g (3 oz) sponge cake or fingers

15 g (½ oz) sultanas

15 g (½ oz) currants

serves 4

To make the custard:

1. Whisk together the eggs, sugar and vanilla essence. Gradually add the milk, whisking all the time.

To make the pudding:

1. Grease and sugar four individual pudding basins or soufflé dishes, decorate the bases with half-cherries (and angelica if liked).

2. Dice the sponge fingers into small 1 cm (½ in.) cubes. Mix with the remaining cherries (chopped), sultanas and currants. Divide this mixture between the four moulds.

3. Strain the custard and pour into the moulds to just below the tops. Allow to stand for 20–30 minutes.

4. Stand the moulds in a baking tin half filled with water, cook in a moderate oven 195°C/380°F/gas mark 5 until the custard is set – approximately 30–40 minutes. Test with a sharp knife blade which should come out clean.

5. Allow to stand for approximately 10 minutes then carefully remove the mould.

6. Serve with more egg custard or hot apricot sauce (as for Soufflé Beignet, page 48).

queen of puddings

ingredients

400 ml (⅔ pt) milk

45 g (1½ oz) butter

2 small eggs

45 g (1½ oz) caster sugar

a handful of cake crumbs

30 g (1 oz) smooth red jam

60 g (2 oz) caster sugar for meringue

serves 4

1. Boil the milk and butter together, separate the eggs and mix the egg yolks with the sugar. Pour on the hot milk and whisk together.

2. Place the cake crumbs in the bottom of an ovenproof dish. Strain the milk mixture onto them and allow to soak for 20–30 minutes.

3. Bake in the oven at 190°C/380°F/gas mark 5 in a tray half filled with water for 30–40 minutes or until set. Allow to cool.

4. Warm the jam and spread it carefully over the set custard.

5. Whisk the egg whites in a clean bowl with a little of the remaining sugar, whisk until stiff and glossy adding the sugar a little at a time.

6. Using a piping bag and a medium piping nozzle, decorate the top of the custard with the meringue. Bake in a hot oven at 235°C/450°F/gas mark 8 until the meringue is golden brown. Serve warm.

old english apple pie

ingredients

For the pastry:

240 g (8½ oz) plain flour

60 g (2 oz) caster sugar

150 g (5 oz) butter

1 egg

For the filling:

30 g (1 oz) butter

480 g (1 lb) peeled and chopped cooking apples

115 g (4 oz) caster sugar

½ tsp fresh grated nutmeg

1 pinch of cinnamon

serves 6

To make the pastry:

1. In a large bowl, combine the flour and caster sugar using your finger tips.

2. Gently rub in the butter until the mixture resembles coarse breadcrumbs.

3. Make a well in the centre and break in the egg, mix carefully to produce a firm but slightly crumbly pastry.

4. Cover with clingfilm and refrigerate for 20 minutes.

To make the filling:

1. In a thick-bottomed saucepan melt the butter and then add the chopped apple.

2. Cook on a low heat under a tight-fitting lid, stir occasionally and cook until soft. Add the sugar, then the nutmeg and cinnamon to taste. Cover and allow to cool completely.

3. When the pastry is rested, divide into two pieces. Cover a buttered heatproof 20 cm (8 in.) pie dish with one half of the pastry rolled thinly.

4. Press gently into the base and sides and trim off any overlapping edges.

5. Prick the pastry base with a fork to prevent it rising. Add the cooked, cooled apple to the centre of the dish and smooth out to the edges.

6. Roll out the remaining pastry, damp the edges of the pie with a little water. Lay the pastry over and trim the edges. Decorate the pastry by pinching the edges between the finger and thumb and make a steam hole in the centre. Bake at 190°C/360°F/gas mark 5 until the pastry is crisp and golden – approximately 25–30 minutes.

Swiss Apple Flan

Ingredients

For the pastry:

30 g (1 oz) self-raising flour

90 g (3 oz) plain flour

15 g (½ oz) sugar

30 g (1 oz) lard or white fat

30 g (1 oz) butter

15 g (½ oz) water

For the filling:

480 g (1 lb) cooking apples peeled, cored and chopped

30 g (1 oz) butter

30 g (1 oz) sultanas

1/2 tsp freshly grated nutmeg

115 g (4 oz) sugar

vanilla essence

1 egg

200 ml (⅓ pt) double cream

60 g (2 oz) apricot jam

To make the pastry:

1. Mix the flours and the sugar. Gently rub in the fats to form coarse crumbs, then add the water and mix to a firm dough. Chill and rest in the refrigerator for 20 minutes.

2. Take a buttered pastry ring and baking sheet or a loose-bottomed flan tin. Roll out the pastry thinly to produce a circle somewhat larger than the ring.

3. Using the rolling pin, lift the pastry over the ring and gently press it down to the base releasing any trapped air. Allow the pastry to hang over the pastry ring edges and refrigerate to allow it to relax.

4. Trim the outer edge of the pastry from the ring and prick the pastry base with a fork.

5. Line the inside of the pastry with silicone paper, fill with baking beans and cook in a pre-heated oven 180°C/355°F/gas mark 4 until the pastry is set but uncoloured.

6. Remove the baking beans and paper.

To make the filling:

1. Cook the apples in a thick-bottomed pan together with the butter under a lid until soft.

2. Add the sultanas, nutmeg and half the sugar and vanilla essence. Allow to cool.

3. Make the egg custard by whisking together the egg, the other half of the sugar and more vanilla essence, then mix in the cream. Drain the cold apple mixture to remove any juices and stir in the egg custard.

4. Spoon this mixture into the pastry case and damp the edge. Cut the leftover pastry into strips to make a trellis to cover the apple mixture.

5. Bake at a low heat 160°C/330°F/gas mark 3 until the apples are set and the pastry trellis is crisp.

6. Heat the apricot jam with a little water and brush between the trellises and over the apple to form a glaze.

serves 4

dutch apple tart

ingredients

For the pastry:

150 g (5½ oz) plain flour

90 g (3 oz) self-raising flour

30 g (1 oz) sugar

60 g (2 oz) butter

60 g (2 oz) lard or white fat

30 ml (1 fl oz) cold water

For the filling:

480 g (1 lb) apples peeled, cored and chopped

30 g (1 oz) butter

grated zest and juice of ½ lemon

170 g (6 oz) caster sugar

60 g (2 oz) sultanas

serves 6

To make the pastry:

1. Place the flours and sugar in a large bowl, add both fats and rub in gently to form coarse crumbs.

2. Add the cold water and mix to a firm dough, cover and refrigerate to rest.

To make the filling:

1. Slowly cook the apples in a thick-bottomed pan with the butter, lemon zest and juice under a tight fitting lid. Add the sugar and sultanas half way through.

2. When cooked to a thick purée, allow the mixture to completely cool.

3. Cover a heatproof pie dish with half of the short pastry using the method given for Old English Apple Pie (see page 26).

4. Add the cold apples and cover with the remaining two thirds of the pastry. Crimp the edge to form a pretty effect, brush with cold water and sprinkle with caster sugar.

5. Make a steam hole in the centre of the tart and bake in a pre-heated oven 190°C/360°F/gas mark 4, until crisp and golden.

6. Serve with lightly whipped cream.

rhubarb crumble

ingredients

For the filling:

480 g (1 lb) of very pink rhubarb

180 g (6 oz) caster sugar

For the crumble:

120 g (4 oz) plain flour

60 g (2 oz) butter

60 g (2 oz) caster sugar

serves 6

To make the filling:

1. Grease an oven-proof pie dish. Trim and wash the rhubarb and cut into 2½ cm (1 in.) pieces and place in the bottom of the dish. Dredge with some the sugar.

To make the crumble:

1. Sift the flour and 30 g (1 oz) of the sugar in a large bowl. Gently rub in the butter to form very coarse crumbs, taking care not to compact the mixture.

2. Scatter this mixture evenly over the rhubarb and sprinkle the remaining caster sugar over the top.

3. Bake in an oven pre-heated to 195°C/380°F/gas mark 5 for approximately 30–40 minutes or until the crumble is golden and crisp.

Honey and pecan tart

ingredients

For the pastry:

120 g (4 oz) plain flour

15 g (½ oz) sugar

60 g (2 oz) butter

1 egg yolk

For the filling:

240 g (8½ oz) honey

150 g (5½ oz) pecans

30 g (1 oz) breadcrumbs

serves 4

To make the pastry:

1. Sift the flour and sugar into a large bowl, and carefully rub in the butter until it resembles coarse breadcrumbs.

2. Add the egg yolk and knead to form a firm dough. Cover with clingfilm and rest in the fridge for 20 minutes.

3. Thoroughly grease a 20 cm (8 in.) flan tin with a loose base and line with the pastry. Leave the pastry edges overhanging until the pastry is well rested to avoid shrinkage, then trim edges.

4. Prick the base with a fork before lining with silicone or baking parchment. Fill with baking beans and cook in a pre-heated oven 205°C/400°F/gas mark 6 for 10–12 minutes.

5. Remove the paper and beans.

To make the filling:

1. Melt the honey in a thick-bottomed pan, add the pecans and simmer for 2 minutes.

2. Scatter the breadcrumbs in the base of the flan and pour the honey and pecan mixture over.

3. Smooth the surface and place in a pre-heated oven 180°C/355°F/gas mark 4 for 20–30 minutes until the pastry is crisp.

4. Serve warm with cream or ice cream.

filo and mincemeat parcels

ingredients

4 sheets of ready-prepared filo pastry

60 g (2 oz) butter (melted)

120 g (4 oz) mincemeat

1 egg yolk

1. Take one sheet of filo pastry and brush with a little melted butter. Fold in half to sandwich the butter, cut this folded sheet in half, and again to form four equal quarters. Carefully butter the top of one quarter.

2. Place a second quarter on top at a slight angle, butter this and repeat the process with a third and fourth square – you should have a filo star shape.

3. Place a spoonful of mincemeat in the centre, brush round the mincemeat with egg yolk whisked with a little water.

4. Draw up the points of the star to form a purse and press the pastry together in the middle to stick. Arrange the pointed tips of the star in a decorative fashion.

5. Brush the parcels with melted butter and bake on a tray in a pre-heated oven 205°C/400°F/gas mark 6 for 10–15 minutes until golden and crisp.

6. Allow to cool slightly before serving with double cream or vanilla ice cream.

serves 4

custard peach flan

ingredients

For the pastry cream:

4 medium egg yolks

20 g (4 oz) sugar

60 g (2 oz) flour

40 ml (⅔ pt) milk

vanilla essence

For the flan pastry:

115 g (4 oz) plain flour

15 g (½ oz) sugar

30 g (1 oz) lard or white fat

30 g (1 oz) butter

1 egg yolk

For the filling:

approximately 8–10 tinned peach halves

serves 4

To make the pastry cream:

1. Whisk egg yolks and sugar, then mix in the flour until smooth.

2. Boil milk and cool slightly. Whisk in the egg mixture. Return to a clean, non-stick pan and bring back to the boil. Pour into a clean bowl, sprinkle a little sugar over the surface and cover tightly with clingfilm until needed.

To make the flan:

1. Mix the sifted flour and sugar in a large bowl. Rub in the fats to produce coarse crumbs.

2. Mix in the egg yolk to form a dough, and allow to rest.

3. Roll out the pastry and line a 20 cm (8 in.) flan tin with a removable base, leaving the edges to overhang until the pastry has rested. Prick the pastry base, trim the edges and line with silicone paper. Fill with baking beans and bake at 200°C/400°F/gas mark 6 for 10–12 minutes until pastry is set.

4. Carefully remove the beans and paper and continue to cook until golden and crisp.

5. Cool slightly and pour in the pastry cream. Arrange the peach halves on top.

6. Chill until required, carefully remove from the flan tin and serve.

raspberry mille feuilles

ingredients

For the shortbread:

120 g (4 oz) butter

70 g (2½ oz) caster sugar

165 g (5½ oz) soft flour

15 g (½ oz) ground rice

For the filling:

300 ml (½ pt) whipping cream

300 g (11 oz) fresh raspberries

small spray of fresh mint leaves

15 g (½ oz) icing sugar

serves 4

To make the shortbread:

1. Cream the butter and sugar until light.

2. Sieve the flour and ground rice into the mixture and blend. Mix to a smooth dough, cover and chill.

3. When cold and firm, divide into two halves and roll each using a dust of rice flour until it is 3 mm (¼ in.) thick.

4. Use a 9 cm (3½ in.) fluted cutter and cut into round. Prick with a fork to prevent rising.

5. Bake on silicone paper at 215°C/420°F/gas mark 7 until golden brown. Store in an airtight tin when completely cold.

To make mille feuilles:

1. Whip the cream until stiff (do not overbeat).

2. Using a piping bag and medium star nozzle, pipe a ball of cream in the centre of the shortbread.

3. Arrange raspberries neatly round the cream and press another shortbread on top.

4. Repeat the process and pipe a neat ball of cream on the top and decorate with a single raspberry and a pair of mint leaves.

5. Place on a serving plate and dust with icing sugar.

apple and cinnamon strudel

ingredients

6 sheets of filo pastry

60 g (2 oz) melted butter

480 g (1 lb) cooking apples washed, peeled and chopped

45 g (1½ oz) bread or cake crumbs

60 g (2 oz) caster sugar

freshly grated nutmeg

cinnamon

30 g (1 oz) apricot jam

serves 6

1. Line the work surface with a large clean cloth, lay three sheets of filo pastry side by side overlapping to form a large rectangle.

2. Brush with melted butter and cover with the remaining three sheets, brush these with melted butter too.

3. Lay a pile of chopped apple along the edge nearest to you but not quite reaching the sides, splash melted butter over the apple, scatter with the sugar, breadcrumbs and freshly grated nutmeg. Dust thickly with cinnamon.

4. Fold the two ends of the filo and roll up the mixture in the cloth to form a large roll. Lift this onto a baking sheet and brush the top with melted butter.

5. Bake in a pre-heated oven 195°C/380°F/gas mark 5 until golden and crisp.

6. Remove from oven and brush with warm apricot jam heated with a little water to make a glaze. Use a sharp serrated knife to cut into slices while still warm.

black cherry crunchy filo flan

ingredients

120 g (4 oz) flour

15 g (½ oz) sugar

90 g (3 oz) butter

30 g (1 oz) lard

1 egg yolk

480 g (1 lb) tinned black cherry pie filling

2 sheets of filo pastry

30 g (1 oz) melted butter

30 g (1 oz) icing sugar

serves 4

1. Mix the flour and sugar in a large bowl. Mix in butter and lard lightly to form coarse breadcrumbs.

2. Mix egg yolk and combine to make firm dough, cover and refrigerate to rest.

3. Roll the chilled mixture thinly and use to line a 20 cm (8 in.) flan tin with a removable base. Prick base with a fork, line with silicone paper and fill with baking beans.

4. Leave the edges overhanging until the pastry has rested for 20 minutes and then trim neatly. Bake in a pre-heated oven for 10–15 minutes at 190°C/365°F/gas mark 4 until the sides are set but not coloured. Remove the silicone and the baking beans.

5. Half fill the flan with the black cherry pie filling.

6. Snip or cut the filo pastry into jagged small pieces. Gently mix with a little melted butter and turn over to thoroughly coat, scatter thickly over the cherries to completely cover.

7. Return to the oven until the flan is cooked and the filo top is golden and crisp. Cool slightly and dust with icing sugar to serve.

fresh strawberry choux buns

ingredients

For the choux pasty:

150 ml (5 fl oz) water

60 g (2 oz) butter

15 g (½ oz) sugar

120 g (4 oz) strong flour (bread flour)

4 eggs

For the filling:

300 ml (10 fl oz) whipping cream

15 g (½ oz) caster sugar

For the coulis:

480 g (1 lb) fresh strawberries

115 g (4 oz) icing sugar

small bunch mint leaves

To make the choux buns:

1. Boil the water in a thick-bottomed pan and add the butter and sugar.

2. When boiling, remove from the heat and stir in the flour.

3. Return to the heat and cook until the mixture comes clearly away from the sides of the pan.

4. Remove and allow the mixture to cool. Beat in the eggs a little at a time.

5. Take a piping bag with a plain tube and pipe out small balls of choux pastry dough on a sheet of silicone paper (allowing for them to double their size during cooking).

6. Bake in a pre-heated oven 235°C/450°F/gas mark 8 for approximately 20 minutes until brown and set, remove and cool.

7. Whip the cream and caster sugar until stiff enough to pipe and, using a piping bag with a small plain nozzle, pierce each bun and fill with cream.

8. Arrange the buns on a plate with the strawberries and dust with icing sugar.

To make fresh strawberry coulis:

1. Divide the strawberries in half, saving the best, most regular-shaped fruit for presentation.

2. Use the ripest fruit to liquidise for the coulis, add 115 g (4 oz) of icing sugar and pass through a fine strain to remove the seeds.

3. Pour the strawberry coulis around the choux buns just before serving.

serves 4

soufflé beignets with Hot Apricot sauce

ingredients

150 ml (5 fl oz) water

60 g (2 oz) butter

15 g (½ oz) sugar

120 g (4 oz) strong flour (bread flour)

4 eggs

225 g (8 oz) apricot jam

30 g (1 oz) icing sugar

serves 4

1. Make the choux pastry as for Fresh Strawberry Choux Buns (page 46).

2. Pre-heat a pan of vegetable oil to moderate frying temperature (approximately 180°C/355°F or when a bread cube dropped in will just start to sizzle and turn pale golden brown).

3. Dip two soup or dessert spoons into the hot oil. Approximately half-fill one spoon with the pastry mixture, using the other spoon to push the dough into the hot fat – each ball should be approximately the size of a walnut.

4. Fry 3–4 at a time allowing them to turn and swell in the hot fat. When they have fully expanded and are crisp and golden brown, lift out onto absorbent paper and dust with icing sugar.

5. Melt the apricot jam with a little water and, when hot, strain to make a sauce. Serve in a sauce boat.

6. Pile the soufflé beignets onto a plate and serve the sauce separately. Dust with icing sugar.

profiteroles with dark chocolate sauce

ingredients

For the choux pastry:

150 ml (5 fl oz) water

60 g (2 oz) butter

15 g (½ oz) sugar

120 g (4 oz) strong flour (bread flour)

4 eggs

For the filling:

200 ml (7 fl oz) whipping cream

30 g (1 oz) caster sugar

vanilla essence

For the dark chocolate sauce:

15 g (½ oz) cornflour or custard powder

280 ml (10 fl oz) milk

15 g (½ oz) butter

45 g (1½ oz) sugar

45 g (1½ oz) dark chocolate (unsweetened)

serves 4

To make the profiteroles:

1. Make the choux pastry as for Fresh Strawberry Choux buns (page 46).

2. Make the profiteroles by piping the cooled choux pastry with a piping bag and a large plain tube into balls approximately half the size of a walnut.

3. Bake in a hot oven 235°C/450°F/gas mark 8 for 15–20 minutes or until crisp and brown. Allow to cool on wire racks.

To make the filling:

1. Whip the cream with the sugar and vanilla until stiff enough to pipe.

2. Use a piping bag and medium sized nozzle to pipe the cream into the profiteroles.

To make the sauce:

1. Mix the cornflour with a little milk.

2. Boil the remaining milk, whisk in the corn flour mixture and add the butter and sugar.

3. Reboil carefully and grate the dark chocolate into the hot (but not boiling) sauce, whisk till smooth.

4. Arrange profiteroles in a pretty dish and pour the chocolate sauce over.

gâteau st Honore

ingredients

½ small packet frozen puff pastry

For the choux pastry:

75 ml (2½ fl oz) water

30 g (1 oz) butter

15 g (½ oz) sugar

60 g (2 oz) strong flour

2 eggs

For the glaze:

115 g (4 oz) sugar

For the filling:

4–5 sponge fingers

2–3 tbsp brandy

200 ml (7 fl oz) whipping cream

30 g (1 oz) caster sugar

vanilla essence

glacé cherries, to decorate

1 tbsp pistachio nuts, chopped

1. Roll out the puff pastry approx 3 mm (¼ in.) thick. Use a pastry ring or small plate to cut the pastry into a circle.

2. Lay the pastry on a sheet of silicone paper and allow to rest for an hour. Prick the base closely with a fork.

3. Make the choux pastry as described on page 46. Using a medium star nozzle, pipe a single ring of choux pastry round the puff pastry. Pipe six separate choux buns on another baking sheet, bake at 205°C/400°F/gas mark 6 until crisp.

To make the glaze:

1. Boil the sugar with 2 tbsp water in a heavy-bottomed pan until the sugar starts to caramelise. Dip the base of the pan quickly into cold water.

To assemble:

1. Dip the bases of the choux buns into the melted sugar and stick them on the top of the choux ring.

2. Use a spoon to dribble melted sugar over the choux pastry edge and over the choux buns to give a decorative edge before the sugar sets.

3. Dice the sponge fingers and soak in the brandy, scatter these on the gâteau base.

4. Whip the cream with the sugar and vanilla and pipe or spoon over the diced sponge fingers to fill the gâteau.

5. Decorate with the cherries and pistachio nuts.

serves 6-8

fresh strawberry and black grape cream trellis

ingredients

½ small packet puff pastry

½ egg mixed with a little water

30 g (1 oz) icing sugar

300 ml (½ pt) whipping cream

30 g (1 oz) caster sugar

vanilla essence

240 g (8½ oz) fresh strawberries

240 g (8½ oz) small seedless black grapes

NB: For this dish you will need a pastry trellis cutter – these come in various types and are available in most kitchen shops, or you could make the dish with thin solid disks of pastry.

1. Roll out the puff pastry to 3 mm (¼ in.) thick and allow to rest for one hour.

2. Use a round cutter or a cup to cut the pastry into disks. Lay each disk on a trellis cutter and cut the disk into a round trellis (you will need three disks per portion).

3. Lay the pastry on silicone paper, brush with egg wash and bake till crisp at 205°C/400°F/ gas mark 6. Remove from the oven and dust with icing sugar, then put back in the oven for 3–4 minutes to glaze.

4. Whip the fresh cream with sugar and vanilla until stiff. Lay the bottom trellis on the serving plate and pipe a ball of cream in the centre. Add strawberries and grapes then place next trellis on top.

5. Repeat this process to form a second layer.

6. On the top, pipe a small ball of cream and decorate with a half strawberry and grape slices, dust with icing sugar.

serves 4

mississippi pecan pie

ingredients

For the pie pastry:

90 g (3 oz) self-raising flour

30 g (1 oz) plain flour

30 g (1 oz) sugar

15 g (½ oz) butter

1 small egg

For the filling:

60 g (2 oz) butter

180 g (6 oz) golden syrup

60 g (2 oz) muscovado sugar

vanilla essence

3 eggs, lightly beaten

150 g (5½ oz) pecans

serves 6

To make the pie case:

1. Make flan pastry by mixing the flours and sugar, gently rub in the butter until the mixture resembles breadcrumbs, mix in the egg to form a firm dough.

2. Cool and rest for an hour.

3. Use the dough to line a flan tin, allow the edges to overhang until rested.

4. Line the pastry with silicone paper and fill with baking beans. Cook in a pre-heated oven 190°C/360°F/gas mark 4 for 10–12 minutes or until the sides have set.

5. Remove the beans and the paper, turn up oven to 200°C/400°F/gas mark 6.

To make the filling:

1. Heat the butter, golden syrup and muscovado sugar until they have melted.

2. Allow to cool, add vanilla the essence and eggs, mix in pecans and pour into flan base.

3. Bake for 30–40 minutes, remove and allow to cool.

Lemon mousse

ingredients

zest of 2 lemons, shredded very finely

240 g (8½ oz) caster sugar

140 g (5 oz) pasteurised egg

15 g (½ oz) gelatine (leaf if possible)

juice of 2 lemons

300 ml (½ pt) whipping cream

15 g (½ oz) chopped pistachios or green rubbed almonds

1. Boil the shredded lemon zest in a little water and 15 g (½ oz) of sugar until soft. Allow to cool.

2. Whisk the pasteurised eggs with the rest of the sugar until thick and white. Melt the gelatine in the lemon juice over heat.

3. Beat the cream until thick, but not to piping consistency. Pour the melted gelatine into the egg mixture and combine, fold in approximately half of the whipped cream.

4. Carefully pour this mixture into four glasses, keeping the edges clean.

5. Beat the remaining cream until stiff and pipe a bulb on the top of each mousse. When set, decorate with the lemon zest and pistachio nuts.

serves 4

chilled vanilla mousse with raspberry coulis

ingredients

300 ml (½ pt) whipping cream

15 g (½ oz) leaf gelatine

150 g (5 ½ oz) pasteurised eggs

120 g (4 oz) caster sugar

vanilla essence

360 g (13 oz) fresh raspberries

60 g (2 oz) icing sugar

fresh mint leaves

serves 6

To make the mousse:

1. Beat the whipping cream until just before piping consistency.

2. Soak the gelatine in cold water, lift out the wet leaves and melt over a gentle heat.

3. Beat the eggs, sugar and vanilla until they are white and stiff, and beat in the melted gelatine.

4. Quickly fold in the whipped cream and spoon into individual greased cake rings. Level the tops and leave to set.

To make the coulis:

1. Select the best raspberries for decoration (about 6–8 for each mousse).

2. Liquidise the remaining fruit and blend in most of the icing sugar. When smooth and shiny, strain to remove the pips.

3. Place each mousse on a plate, run a small knife blade round the mould and lift off carefully.

4. Arrange the raspberries on the top of each mousse and pour the raspberry coulis around the outside, decorate with a mint leaf.

fresh strawberry soufflé with strawberry and basil compote

ingredients

For the soufflé:

430 g (15 oz) fresh strawberries

juice of 1 lemon

60 g (2 oz) caster sugar

30 g (1 oz) gelatine

60 g (2 oz) egg whites –
approx. 2 eggs

300 ml (10 fl oz) whipping cream

For the compote:

30 ml (1 fl oz) raspberry vinegar

15 g (½ oz) sugar

45 g (1½ oz) strawberries

2 tbsp chopped basil leaves

serves 6

To make the soufflé:

1. Set aside four small neat strawberries for garnish and roughly chop the rest.

2. Heat the lemon juice with 30 g (1 oz) of sugar and add the strawberries.

3. Gently soak the gelatine in cold water and add to the hot strawberries. Liquidise and keep warm.

4. Whisk the egg whites and remaining caster sugar over a bowl of hot water until the mixture is hot to the touch (approximately 70°C/160°F). Remove from the heat and whisk with an electric whisk until cold.

5. Beat the cream lightly and fold the meringue into the strawberries followed by the cream.

6. Line the outside of six soufflé moulds with silicone paper and hold in place with string or an elastic band.

7. Pour the mixture into the mould and refrigerate until set. Remove the paper and place half a fresh strawberry on the top of each.

To make the compote:

1. Heat the vinegar and add the sugar. Neatly dice the strawberries and add.

2. Remove from the heat and add the basil.

3. Serve flooded around the soufflé.

gooseberry fool

ingredients

480 g (1 lb) fresh green gooseberries

240 g (8½ oz) sugar

750 ml (1½ pt) water

280 ml (10 fl oz) milk

30 g (1 oz) sugar

30 g (1 oz) cornflour

140 ml (5 fl oz) whipping cream

serves 4

1. Top and tail the gooseberries, then place in a thick-bottomed pan with the sugar and water. Cover with foil, place on a moderate heat and poach.

2. When the gooseberries are just poached but still firm, remove four small just-cooked fruits and cook the rest until soft. Purée and allow to cool.

3. Add a little of the milk to the cornflour, mix to a smooth batter and add the sugar. In a separate pan, boil the milk and whisk it into the mixture. Return this mix to the pan and bring to the boil, whisking all the time.

4. Pour this mixture into the purée and strain into four clean glasses.

5. Whisk the cream and pipe onto the top, decorate with a lightly poached gooseberry.

NB: You could add one or two drops of apple cream colour to the mixture to produce a very soft green gooseberry colour.

rHubarb fool

ingredients

480 g (1 lb) rhubarb (very pink)

120 g (4 oz) sugar

750 ml (1½ pt) water (hot)

300 ml (½ pt) whipping cream

4 mint leaves

serves 4

1. Carefully wash the rhubarb stalks, trim any discoloured ends and cut into 2½ cm (1 in.) pieces.

2. Place into a pie dish, scatter with sugar and add the hot water. Cover with foil and place in a pre-heated oven 180°C/355°F/gas mark 4, cook for approximately 10 minutes.

3. Remove foil and select approximately eight neat pink rhubarb pieces to use as garnish.

4. Return rhubarb to the oven and continue to cook until soft (approximately 20 minutes), cool slightly and liquidise.

5. Beat the cream until nearly stiff and when the rhubarb is cold, fold half of the cream into the rhubarb.

6. Continue to whip the remaining half of the cream to piping consistency, allow the fool to set in pretty glasses, pipe a rosette of cream on each and decorate with a poached rhubarb stick and a mint leaf.

crème caramel

ingredients

For the caramel:

60 g (2 oz) caster sugar

90 ml (3 fl oz) water

For the custard:

4 eggs

115 g (4 oz) sugar

vanilla essence

570 ml (20 fl oz) milk

serves 4

To make the caramel:

1. Lightly grease four individual pudding moulds or soufflé dishes.

2. Make the caramel by boiling the sugar with 60 ml (2 fl oz) of the water in a thick-bottomed pan. Very carefully cook until the sugar turns a golden amber colour. Remove from heat and add the last 30 ml (1 fl oz) of the water (beware of steam!).

3. Return the pan to the heat and reboil while stirring. Divide the caramel between the four moulds. Allow to stand and form a skin.

To make the custard:

1. Whisk the eggs with the sugar and vanilla essence and add the milk. Strain through a fine strainer onto the caramel.

2. Stand the moulds in a roasting tray and surround with water. Cook in a moderate oven 195°C/380°F/gas mark 5 for 30–40 minutes or until set.

3. Allow to cool and thoroughly chill in the refrigerator.

4. To serve, loosen the edges of the mould with a sharp knife and up-end on to a plate. Tap to unmould then pour the caramel over the top to surround the dish.

blueberry crème brûlée

ingredients

570 ml (20 fl oz) double cream

115 g (4 oz) caster sugar

5 egg yolks

vanilla essence

60 g (2 oz) fresh blueberries

60 g (2 oz) demerara sugar

1. Boil the cream. Whisk the caster sugar with the egg yolks and vanilla, then pour on the boiling cream and whisk.

2. Grease soufflé moulds. Divide the blueberries between the moulds and pour on the cream mixture.

3. Place in a roasting tray half filled with water. Bake in a low oven 145°C/290°F/gas mark 1 cook for 15–20 minutes until just set. Do not allow to boil.

4. Allow to cool then chill. Cover the top of the mixture with demerara sugar and place the brûlée under a very hot grill until the sugar is melted and bubbling. Serve immediately.

serves 6

cranachan cream

ingredients

60 g (2 oz) medium oats

4 tbsp (60 ml) clear honey

3 tbsp (45 ml) whisky

900 ml (30 fl oz) double cream

360 g (12 oz) raspberries

mint sprigs

serves 4

1. Spread the oats on a grill tray and either bake in a moderate oven 195°C/380°F/gas mark 5 until crisp (5–6 minutes), or lightly grill to colour. Leave to cool.

2. Mix the clear honey with the whisky and warm through gently and allow to cool. Whip the cream in a large bowl until lightly beaten. Gently fold in the honey mix and the oats.

3. Using four glasses, take a piping bag and pipe a layer of the cream mixture in each glass. Add a layer of raspberries and continue adding layers of cream and fruit until full.

4. Finish the glasses with one or two raspberries and the mint leaves.

poached pears with hot chocolate sauce and almonds

ingredients

For the pears:

4 firm cooking pears with stalks

juice of one lemon

570 ml (20 fl oz) water

300 g (10½ oz) sugar

1 bay leaf

2 cloves

half a cinnamon stick

15 g (½ oz) flaked almonds toasted

For the chocolate sauce:

250 ml (9 fl oz) water

240 g (8½ oz) caster sugar

140 g (5 oz) plain chocolate

45 g (1½ oz) cocoa powder

15 g (½ oz) cornflour

150 ml (¼ pt) single cream

1. Peel the pears and leave the stalk in place. Use a melon baller to remove the core from the base, level off with a knife so the pear will stand. Brush with lemon juice.

2. Make a syrup from the water, sugar, bay leaf, cloves and cinnamon stick. Boil and allow to simmer for 2–3 minutes.

3. Add the peeled pears and the lemon juice. Cover the pears with foil and allow to simmer gently until the pears are just cooked (approximately 15–20 minutes). Test with the point of a knife, leave in the syrup to cool.

To make the sauce:

1. Place the water, half the sugar and the chocolate in a saucepan. Bring slowly to the boil.

2. In a separate bowl whisk the cocoa powder, remaining sugar, cornflour and cream together to form a smooth cream. Pour some of the boiling mixture onto this and mix together.

3. Pour this mixture back into the chocolate in the pan and whisk until the sauce boils and thickens.

4. Spoon the chocolate sauce over the pears. Serve with ice cream and scatter with toasted almonds.

serves 4

freʃH pineapple poacHed in wHite rum ʃyrup

ingredientʃ

zest and juice of 2 oranges

zest and juice of 1 lime

1 medium-sized fresh pineapple

60 g (2 oz) butter

90 g (3 oz) demerara sugar

½ tsp whole green peppercorns

60 ml (2 fl oz) dry white wine

4 tbsp white rum

serves 4

1. Thinly peel the oranges and lime, squeeze carefully to produce the maximum juice. Finely shred the orange and lime zest, blanche for one minute in boiling water and strain.

2. Top and tail the pineapple (retain the pineapple top with foliage) and peel off the rough skin. Use a pineapple corer to remove the core. With a sharp knife, slice into eight even slices.

3. Heat a large non-stick frying pan and add the butter and demerara sugar. Cook until the sugar melts, add the orange and lime zest and the green peppercorns. Cook for one minute, add the juices and the white wine, allow to boil.

4. Add the pineapple slices and cook carefully on one side for 2–3 minutes. Turn over and repeat on the other side, add the white rum and toss the pineapple in the syrup.

5. Stand the pineapple top carefully in the middle of a large pretty dish or plate, overlap the poached pineapple rings round the outside.

6. Adjust the consistency of the sauce by boiling it; if it is too thin allow to reduce, if too thick, add a little more orange juice or white wine. Pour the syrup over the pineapple slices allowing it to flow to the edges of the dish. Serve warm with balls of vanilla ice cream.

poached fresh strawberries with black pepper syrup and vanilla ice cream

ingredients

480 g (1 lb) firm fresh strawberries

60 g (2 oz) butter

90 g (3 oz) caster sugar

½ tsp crushed black peppercorns

juice of 2 lemons

60 g (2 oz) water

1 fresh vanilla pod

4 balls of vanilla ice cream

serves 6

1. Wash and halve the strawberries cutting any larger ones into quarters.

2. In a non-stick frying pan, melt the butter and add the sugar. Allow the sugar to melt and turn to a pale gold colour, then add the pepper and the lemon juice and boil.

3. Add the water and the vanilla pod. Cook to form a thin syrup, then add the strawberries and poach for 1–2 minutes.

4. Lift out the strawberries with a slotted spoon and arrange in four bowls. Remove the vanilla pod from the syrup and split it lengthways with the blade of a knife, scraping the vanilla seeds back into the syrup.

5. Reboil the syrup until it starts to thicken and pour over the strawberries. Place a ball of vanilla ice cream in each bowl.

galia melon
fruit salad basket

ingredients

2 ripe galia melons (you can also use charentais)

1 red eating apple

1 green eating apple

8 medium strawberries

60 g (2 oz) raspberries

30–60g (1–2 oz) of redcurrants, blueberries, grapes, cherries or whatever fresh fruit is available

juice of 1 lemon

60 g (2 oz) sugar

115 ml (4 fl oz) water

serves 4

1. With a sharp paring knife cut each melon into two equal halves van dyke style (this will give a serrated edge).

2. Use a melon baller or scoop to remove the seeds and cut the flesh of the melon into balls. Do not cut too close to the skin of the melon. Use the scoop to scrape down the inside of the melon shell, leave the debris on the bottom.

3. Prepare the remaining fruit: cut the apples into quarters and remove the cores. Quarter the strawberries, arrange the fruit and melon balls in the shell.

4. Brush the apple slices with lemon juice to prevent discolouration. Use the remaining lemon juice, the sugar and water to make a syrup. Heat until the sugar has dissolved and then chill.

5. Use the syrup to top up the melon shells. Serve each melon shell in a bowl, with double cream in a sauce boat.

Hunza Apricots with orange and pistachios

ingredients

240 g (8½ oz) Hunza dried apricots

115 g (4 oz) prunes

60 g (2 oz) sultanas

140 ml (5 fl oz) orange juice

30 g (1 oz) toasted pinenuts

30 g (1 oz) roughly chopped pistachio nuts

1 measure of orange liqueur (to taste)

the seeds from one pomegranate
(if available)

2 oranges cut into segments

30 g (1 oz) flaked almonds

serves 4

1. Place the apricots, prunes and sultanas in a large bowl and cover with orange juice. Allow to soak overnight.

2. Transfer to a thick-bottomed pan and very gently bring to the boil. Simmer for 10–15 minutes allow to cool in the liquid.

3. Transfer to a serving dish and sprinkle with the pinenuts, flaked almonds, pistachios and liqueur.

4. Cut the pomegranates in half, remove the seeds and scatter them over the top. Decorate with orange segments.

5. Serve with thick Greek yogurt or crème fraîche.

strawberries romanoff

ingredients

zest and juice from 1 orange

480 g (1 lb) strawberries

orange liqueur

45 g (1½ oz) icing sugar

300 ml (½ pt) double cream

2 tbsp brandy

1. Peel the zest of the orange very thinly and shred with a sharp knife. Squeeze the juice out.

2. Place the strawberries in a large bowl retaining four for garnish. Pour the orange juice and half the zest over the strawberries and add the orange liqueur to taste.

3. Scatter with half the icing sugar and mix. Cover with clingfilm and chill for one hour.

4. Whip the cream in a separate bowl until nearly stiff, mix in the remaining sugar and the brandy and finish beating.

5. Take four sundae glasses and half fill with the strawberries, top with the brandy cream, decorate with the remaining strawberries and orange shreds.

serves 4

eton mess

ingredients

480 g (1 lb) strawberries

15 g (½ oz) caster sugar

1 tbsp cherry brandy

5–6 small meringues

300 ml (½ pt) whipping cream

small bunch mint

serves 4

1. Hull and wash the strawberries, setting aside four neat ones.

2. Cut the rest of the fruit into 6–8 segments, depending on size. Add the sugar and cherry brandy and mix together. Crush the meringue roughly and add to the strawberries.

3. Whip the cream to soft peaks and spoon over the strawberry mixture, gently fold together. Spoon the mixture into bowls and decorate with the remaining strawberries and the mint leaves.

freſh peacH melba

ingredientſ

2 very ripe peaches

300 g (10½ oz) ripe raspberries

juice of half a lemon to taste

30–60 g (1–2 oz) icing sugar to taste

four balls of vanilla ice cream

150 ml (¼ pt) whipped cream

1 tbsp toasted almonds

4 mint leaves

1. Use a sharp knife to cut around the lateral line of the peach down to the stone. Gently twist to remove stone.

2. Drop the peaches into boiling water for 8–10 seconds, lift out and place in cold water. Slip the skin off, keeping the peach halves intact.

3. Liquidise the raspberries with a little lemon juice and icing sugar to taste. Strain carefully to remove the seeds.

4. To serve, place a ball of vanilla ice cream in a glass and gently press a peach half on top. Carefully spoon the fresh raspberry sauce over the peach. Repeat for the other portions.

5. Garnish with the whipped cream, toasted almonds and mint leaves.

serves 4

ice cream strawberry shortcake

ingredients

To make the shortcake:

115 g (4 oz) butter

70 g (2½ oz) caster sugar

165 g (5½ oz) plain flour

15 g (½ oz) rice flour

To make the filling:

approximately 4 balls of vanilla ice cream

480 g (1 lb) strawberries

serves 4

For the shortcake:

1. Cream the butter and sugar together until light.

2. Sieve in the flour and rice flour and add to the butter mix. Mix together to make a smooth paste, cover and chill.

3. Divide the mixture into eight even-sized balls and roll on sheets of silicone paper approximately 6 cm (2½ in.) Bake in a pre-heated oven 200°C/400°F/gas mark 6 until crisp and golden. As soon as they are baked dredge with a little more caster sugar whilst still hot.

For the filling:

1. When the shortcake is cold, sandwich with small balls of vanilla ice cream scooped with a melon baller.

2. Alternate with halves of small strawberries, decorate the tops with more ice cream and strawberries.

baked blueberry cheesecake

ingredients

150 g (5 oz) crushed digestive biscuits

60 g (2 oz) butter (melted)

170 g (6 oz) cottage cheese

150 g (5 oz) natural yogurt

1 tsp plain flour

15 g (½ oz) caster sugar

1 egg plus 1 egg white

juice and grated zest of half a lemon

200 g (7 oz) blueberries

mint leaves

1. Grease and line a 2½ cm (1 in.) sponge tin. Mix the digestive biscuits, and melted butter together and spoon into the tin. Chill until firm.

2. Place the cottage cheese in a food processor and process till smooth.

3. Mix in the yogurt, flour, sugar, egg and egg white. Stir gently, mix in the lemon zest and juice. Lastly fold in the blueberries, saving a few for decoration.

4. Pour the mixture onto the biscuit base and bake in a pre-heated oven 180°C/355°F/gas mark 4 for 30–35 minutes or until just set. Turn off the oven and leave for another 30 minutes.

5. Run a knife around the cheesecake and carefully turn out onto a serving plate and decorate with the remaining blueberries and mint leaves.

serves 4

rhubarb and ginger ice cream

ingredients

600 g (1¼ lb) rhubarb very pink,
cut into small pieces

90 g (3 oz) caster sugar

300 ml (½ pt) single cream

4 egg yolks

30 g (1 oz) ginger syrup

1 walnut-sized piece of stem ginger

fresh mint leaves

serves 6

1. Place the rhubarb and sugar in a thick-bottomed pan. Add 2–3 tbsp of water and cover with a tight-fitting lid.

2. Cook over a very low heat until just cooked but still firm. Remove six neat pieces for garnish and continue cooking the remainder. When soft, remove from the heat and liquidise.

3. Place the single cream, egg yolks and the ginger syrup in a bowl over a pan of simmering water and beat until the mixture thickens.

4. Finely slice and shred the ginger, put half aside for garnish, fold the other half and the rhubarb purée into the custard-like mixture.

5. Place in an electric ice cream machine (if available) and freeze, or put into a freezer tray and slowly freeze until firm. Stir several times during the freezing process to break up the ice crystals and to make smooth.

6. When frozen, scoop into individual serving dishes and decorate with a rhubarb stick, a mint leaf and a few shreds of ginger.

strawberry ginger snaps

ingredients

60 g (2 oz) butter

60 g (2 oz) caster sugar

60 g (2 oz) golden syrup

60 g (2 oz) flour

½ tsp ground ginger

half a lemon

300 ml (½ pt) double cream

15 g (½ oz) sugar

1 tbsp brandy

240 g (8½ oz) strawberries

serves 4

1. Melt the butter, sugar and syrup in a small pan. Stir in the flour and ginger, add the grated rind of the half lemon and 1 tbsp of the juice.

2. Place 12 tablespoons of the mixture well spaced on silicone paper and press out. Bake at 180°C/355°F/gas mark 4 for 8–10 minutes until golden. Allow to cool slightly and slide off the paper onto cooling wires.

3. Whip the cream with the 15 g (½ oz) icing sugar and the brandy until soft.

4. Spoon fresh cream into the middle of one ginger snap, surround with fresh strawberries and sandwich with a second ginger snap. Repeat with a third and decorate the top with cream and a single strawberry.

5. Repeat the process to produce three more strawberry ginger snaps.

brandy snap baskets filled with black cherry cream

ingredients

For the brandy snaps:

60 g (2 oz) golden syrup

60 g (2 oz) caster sugar

60 g (2 oz) butter

60 g (2 oz) flour

½ tsp ground ginger

grated zest of half a lemon

1 tsp brandy

For the filling:

425 g (15 oz) tin black cherries

300 ml (½ pt) double cream

30 g (1 oz) icing sugar

2 tbsp cherry brandy

fresh mint leaves

serves 6

To make the brandy snaps:

1. Melt the golden syrup, caster sugar and butter. Mix in the flour, ginger, lemon zest and brandy.

2. Pre-heat the oven to 180°C/355°F/gas mark 4. Spoon the mixture into walnut-sized pieces and place on to silicone paper two at a time, space well. Press to spread, slightly bake for 8–10 minutes until golden. Leave to cool for a few moments, drape each one over an individual pudding basin or small cup. Allow to cool.

To make the filling:

1. Chop or liquidise one third of the black cherries. Beat the double cream to soft peaks, fold in the icing sugar, cherry brandy and the puréed black cherries.

2. Continue to beat until stiff. To serve, spoon into the brandy snap baskets and top with the whole cherries. Add a mint leaf to decorate.

Lemon cheesecake with strawberries and blueberries

ingredients

150 g (5 oz) digestive biscuits (crushed)

60 g (2 oz) crushed hazelnuts

90 g (3 oz) melted butter

360 g (12 oz) curd cheese

60 g (2 oz) caster sugar

3 eggs, separated

freshly grated zest and juice of 1 lemon

15 g (½ oz) gelatine (powdered)

300 ml (½ pt) whipping cream

240 g (8½ oz) strawberries

115 g (4 oz) blueberries

serves 6

1. Mix the digestive biscuits, crushed hazelnuts and melted butter together and spoon into a 20 cm (8 in.) stainless cake ring on a serving plate. Chill until firm.

2. In a bowl, heat the curd cheese with the sugar, egg yolks and lemon zest. Dissolve the gelatine with the lemon juice over heat and stir into the cheese mixture.

3. Fold in the lightly beaten cream. Whisk the egg whites until stiff and fold in.

4. Cut the strawberries in half and stand up around the cake ring, spoon in the cheesecake mixture and press out to the sides. Level off, cover and chill until set.

5. Arrange half strawberries around top edge and fill the centre with blueberries. When required, slide a sharp knife around the edge and remove the ring.

vacherin à la russe

ingredients

570 ml (20 fl oz) double cream

60 g (2 oz) caster sugar

30 g (1 oz) rum

approximately 10–12 ready-made
meringue nests or broken meringues

12 pineapple rings (tinned)

240 g (8½ oz) black grapes

60 g (2 oz) dark chocolate

serves 6

1. Beat the cream with the sugar and rum until stiff.

2. Place a 20 cm (8 in.) cake ring on a serving plate
   and put a spoonful of the cream in the middle and
   spread out.

3. Place a layer of broken meringues on top. Finely
   chop four pineapple rings and scatter over the
   meringues. Cover with cream and sandwich with a
   second layer of meringues.

4. Cover the second layer of meringue with cream and
   smooth out. Cut pineapple rings in half and use to
   decorate the top along with the black grapes.

5. To serve, use a sharp knife to remove ring. Melt the
   chocolate in a bowl over a pan of hot water and
   dribble over the sides of the vacherin to finish.

fruits of the forest meringue nest

ingredients

3 egg whites

240 g (8 ½ oz) caster sugar

480 g (1 lb) mixed berries (raspberries, currants, blackberries, strawberries or a packet of frozen mixed red fruit)

300 ml (½ pt) whipping cream

30 g (1 oz) icing sugar

serves 6

1. Using a spotlessly clean bowl with no traces of grease, mix the egg whites (which have no trace of yolk) with the caster sugar.

2. Place over a bowl of simmering water, ensuring the base of the bowl does not touch the water. Use a whisk to mix the sugar and whites until the sugar has dissolved and the egg white is warm to the touch, about 10 minutes.

3. Remove from the heat and beat with an electric whisk until cold, thick and glossy. Use a piping bag and medium star nozzle, pipe in a spiral on a silicone paper to produce rings of approximately 7 ½ cm (3 in.) in diameter.

4. Pipe a border around the outside of the ring. Pre-heat the oven to 170°C/335°F/gas mark 3 and bake the ring for approximately 15 minutes. Turn off the oven and leave the meringues in overnight to dry.

5. Beat the cream and when the meringues are cold, pipe a border of cream around the outside. Arrange the mixed fruit in the centre and dust with icing sugar.

fresh raspberry meringue roulade with dark chocolate sauce

ingredients

For the roulade:

4 egg whites

pinch of salt

200 g (7 oz) caster sugar

1 tsp white vinegar

1 tsp vanilla essence

2 tsp cornflour

300 ml (½ pt) whipping cream – beaten till stiff

240 g (8½ oz) ripe raspberries

For the chocolate sauce:

115 g (4 oz) dark chocolate

2–3 tbsp strong black coffee

150 ml (¼ pt) double cream

serves 6

To make the roulade:

1. Place the egg whites and a pinch of salt in a clean bowl and whisk with an electric mixer until stiff. Gradually add 170 g (6 oz) of the caster sugar, beating until stiff and glossy.

2. Fold in the vinegar, vanilla essence and cornflour, spread the mixture evenly on a swiss roll tray lined with silicone paper. Bake for 15 minutes at 170°C/335°F/gas mark 3 or until firm to the touch. Turn over onto a clean silicone paper scattered with the remaining caster sugar.

3. Allow to rest for five minutes, peel off the paper and roll up with the fresh piece of paper to form a swiss roll.

4. Allow to cool and unroll, fill with whipped cream and scatter with the raspberries.

5. Re-roll the meringue using the paper, again transfer to a serving plate decorated with a few raspberries.

To make the sauce:

1. Melt the chocolate over a pan of hot water, stir in the coffee and the double cream to make a dark rich sauce. Surround the roulade with the sauce to serve.

kiwi and toasted almond pavlova

ingredients

4 egg whites

pinch of salt

240 g (8 ½ oz) caster sugar

1 tsp white vinegar

1 tsp cornflour

For the filling:

400 ml (⅔ pt) double cream

60 g (2 oz) flaked almonds

15 g (½ oz) icing sugar

6 kiwi fruit peeled and sliced

serves 6

1. Beat egg whites in a clean bowl with the salt until they form stiff peaks. Gradually beat in the caster sugar until smooth and glossy, fold in the white vinegar and cornflour.

2. Draw a 23 cm (9 in.) circle on silicone paper and spread the meringue evenly over the circle. Smooth with a palette knife and bake in a pre-heated oven 140°C/275°F/gas mark 1 for 10 minutes. Reduce heat to 100°C/225°F, cook for 45 minutes and turn off.

3. Allow to stand for approximately one hour, transfer to a serving plate and cool.

To make the filling:

1. Whip the cream and spread half of it over the meringue.

2. Lightly toast the flaked almonds until golden brown, dust with icing sugar and glaze under the grill for a few seconds.

3. Decorate the meringue with the sliced kiwi, remaining double cream and flaked almonds.

vanilla and butterscotch vacherin

ingredients

approximately 16 individual meringue cases

280 ml (10 fl oz) whipping cream

4 balls of vanilla ice cream

115 g (4 oz) butter

115 g (4 oz) demerara sugar

280 ml (10 fl oz) double cream

1. Break up four meringue cases into small pieces in a shallow dish. Beat the whipping cream until stiff.

2. Place the balls of ice cream in six individual meringue cases and place a second meringue case on top of each, pressing gently to flatten. Use a palette knife to spread a little cream around the sides of the double meringues.

3. Roll the sides in broken meringue, place in the deep freeze until needed.

To make the sauce:

1. Melt the butter and demerara sugar in a thick bottomed pan, simmer gently until the sugar has melted and the sauce begins to thicken and becomes dark brown and caramelised.

2. Remove from heat and add the double cream carefully (the sauce will splutter and appear curdled).

3. Reboil and simmer gently until the sauce is smooth and honey coloured. Remove from the heat and allow to cool (at this point the sauce will be very hot and dangerous to touch).

To serve:

1. Use the remaining whipping cream and a piping bag to pipe a circle of cream around the top of each meringue.

2. Fill the top of the meringue with cold butterscotch sauce and serve.

serves 6

floating islands

ingredients

For the meringue:

3 medium egg whites

1 pinch of salt

170 g (6 oz) caster sugar

For the custard:

570 ml (20 fl oz) milk

vanilla essence

4 egg yolks

60 g (2 oz) caster sugar

15g (½ oz) toasted flaked almonds

serves 4

To make the meringue:

1. In a very clean bowl, beat the egg whites with a pinch of salt until they form soft peaks.

2. Add the caster sugar a little at a time, beating continuously until thick and glossy.

3. Boil the milk and the vanilla essence and allow to simmer in a thick bottomed pan.

4. Using two tablespoons, shape the meringues into large eggs passing from spoon to spoon. Then place them into the simmering milk and poach for approximately 5–6 mins before turning over and poaching the other side.

5. When completely cooked, carefully lift out onto a plate and chill.

To make the custard:

1. Ensure you still have approximately 570 ml (20 fl oz) of boiling milk – if not, top up and reboil. Whisk the egg yolks and the caster sugar until fluffy and pour onto the boiling milk, whisking all the time.

2. Return the mixture to the pan and stir over gentle heat until the mixture coats the back of the spoon (do not reboil). Pass the mixture through a fine strainer.

3. Divide the sauce between four plates and pile the poached meringues in the middle. Scatter flaked almonds onto each portion.

Lemon and raspberry sorbet bombe

ingredients

2 eggs (separated)

240 g (8½ oz) caster sugar

300 ml (½ pt) double cream

finely grated zest of 2 lemons

juice of 3 lemons

170 g (6 oz) raspberries

grated rind and juice of 1 orange

a few fresh raspberries to decorate

serves 6-8

1. In a large clean bowl whisk half the egg whites until stiff, whisk in half the sugar and the egg yolks.

2. Beat half the cream until thick, add the lemon zest and juice. Fold into the egg mixture and pour into a freezer-proof bowl. Freeze until firm.

3. Place the raspberries in a saucepan with the remaining sugar, orange rind and juice, poach for 4–5 minutes.

4. Lift out half the raspberries and set aside, strain the remaining fruit and chill. Whip the remaining cream until thick and fold in the purée, followed by the raspberries. Whisk the remaining egg whites till stiff and fold into the mixture, cover and freeze until firm.

5. Chill a 1.25 l (40 fl oz) bombe mould or pudding basin. Line with the lemon and ice cream, cover and freeze for one hour. Fill the centre with raspberry ice cream and freeze until firm.

6. To serve, dip the bowl into water for a few seconds and un-mould onto a plate. Cut into wedges and decorate with raspberries and orange zest.

chocolate meringues with walnut and cinnamon cream

ingredients

5 egg whites

pinch of salt

360 g (12 oz) caster sugar

225 g (8 oz) dark chocolate

300ml (½ pt) whipping cream

ground cinnamon to taste

4 walnut halves

serves 4

1. Beat the egg whites and salt until they form soft peaks. Gradually beat in the sugar until stiff and shiny.

2. Line a baking sheet with silicone paper. Use a piping bag with a medium star nozzle to pipe the meringue out into nests approximately 9 cm (3½ in.) in a spiral, starting in the centre. The mixture should produce four nests. Bake in a pre-heated oven 110°C/225°F/gas mark ¼ for approximately 2½ hours or until crisp.

3. Melt the chocolate over a bowl of warm water and spoon a little into the base of each nest. Allow to set.

4. Beat the cream until half whipped, feed in most of the remaining chocolate and flavour with cinnamon.

5. To serve, spoon the mixture into the meringue cases, decorate with the walnut halves and dribble the remaining chocolate over the sides.